Spirits that Fight against the Kingdom of God

By Overseer, Prophet Daniel Powell, Sr.

Copyright © 2023 Daniel Powell, Sr.

All rights reserved.

No part of this book may be reproduced, or stored in a retrieval system, or transmitted in any form or by any means, electronic, mechanical, photocopying, recording, or otherwise, without the express written permission of the publisher.

The opinions expressed in this book are those of the author and does not constitute medical advice or legal advice. Any similarities to real persons other than the author, living or dead, are coincidental and not intended by the author.

The author is an ordained minister and thereby cites The Holy Bible in a sermonic and instructional capacity. All scriptures and biblical citations are intended for and reproduced for ministerial education purposes. The author makes no intellectual property claims regarding any specific translations of The Holy Bible cited herein.

ISBN-13: 979-8-218-14623-8

Printed in the United States of America

Contents

Dedication	4
Forewords	5
SPIRIT OF ABOMINATION	8
SPIRIT OF ANANIAS AND SAPPHIRA	9
SPIRIT OF ANTINOMIANISM	13
SPIRIT OF ANXIETY	19
SPIRIT OF APOSTASY	22
SPIRIT OF NECESSITY / COMPULSION GIVING	24
SPIRIT OF DOUBT	29
SPIRIT OF FAMILIAR SPIRITS	30
SPIRIT OF FEAR	31
SPIRIT OF JEALOUSY	32
SPIRIT OF LABAN	34
SPIRIT OF LAWLESSNESS	35
SPIRIT OF LILITH (OWL)	40
SPIRIT OF LOW SELF-ESTEEM	41
SPIRIT OF NAGGING	43
SPIRIT OF OSIRIS	44
SPIRIT OF PROMISCUITY	45
SPIRIT OF SCOFFER	47
SPIRIT OF SCHISM	49
SPIRIT OF SELF-PITY	50
SPIRIT OF SELF-CENTEREDNESS	51

SPIRIT OF SLOTHFULNESS	57
SPIRIT OF TRUTH AND SPIRIT OF ERROR	58
SPIRIT OF YOGA	61
WITCHCRAFT, SEDUCING SPIRITS	64
HOROSCOPE or HORROR-SCOPE	75
GOD'S THOUGHTS AND HIS WAYS ARE NOT LIKE OURS	79
About the Author	82

Dedication

Hallelujah to the King of all kings, and the Lord of all lords! I give all glory, honor, and praise unto Him. He is the Ancient of Days and the Savior of my soul. To my Lord and my King, who is my rock. To Him be all the glory. I bless His name. I give honor to the Holy Spirit, my guide and my teacher, and embrace the wisdom of God, by which we love truth and righteousness.

To my dear wife and best friend, Prophetess Esther Powell, through you, I experienced incomparable love. Thank you for your spiritual support, steadfast love, and constant encouragement to fulfill all that God has ordained for me to be. Hallelujah to the Most High God!

Forewords

In regards to my loving husband and my very best friend of 45 years, I met the author, Overseer Prophet Daniel Powell, Sr., approximately 45 years ago. We got married in Miami, Florida on December 20th of 1980. At that time, neither one of us knew the Lord, but as time went on, I got saved, and got to know the Lord, and then Prophet Daniel Powell, Sr. also received salvation from the Lord. Through this journey, I saw the man of God, totally transformed overnight.

I saw him surrender his will to the Lord and about a year or two later, we moved to Valdosta, Georgia to be under the covering and leadership of the Head Apostle Kathy Kinchen and K.K. International Ministries. This is where everything began for us in ministry. It is so fitting that the man of God decided to write a book concerning the spirits that fight against the kingdom of God.

During our journey, we have experienced many spirits that fight against the kingdom of God or that fight against people as a whole and I can truly attest to the fact that I have seen this man of God evolve in such a beautiful way. I always say who knows you better than the person that you are with every single day so I guess you can say I am a witness of what the Lord has done for him in his life, in our lives, and how fitting it is, that he can explain and elaborate on the spirits that fight against the kingdom of God, and how important it is to be able to identify the spirits and to deal with the strong man. **"But if I cast out**

demons by the Spirit of God, surely the kingdom of God has come upon you. Or how can one enter a strong man's house and plunder his goods, unless he first binds the strong man? And then he will plunder his house" (Matthew 12:28-29, NKJV).

I also must say in this walk we do come up against so many different spirits. I have seen this man evolve in such a great way from becoming a deacon, to an evangelist, to a prophet, and now to an overseer that oversees Faith & Works Ministries, Heaven to Earth Worship Center, Open Heaven Academy, and many churches nationally and internationally. I have seen the man of God, counsel many leaders and members in general, helping them to be able to also overcome the spirits that fight against the kingdom of God.

One thing that I do know from watching his life and being a part of it is that he's more than qualified to have written this book. As a witness firsthand, I feel like I am a part of it because certain spirits we've had to deal with in our personal lives, and I've seen the Lord get the victory in every part. In conclusion, I thought it fitting just to say something about the author and he is truly a true man of God. He is an eagle eye prophet, he is one that stays in tune with the spirit, but if I had to say anything, I would say he's a man that walks in the spirit of humility, and has an ear to hear what the Spirit of the Lord has to say unto the churches.

From your loving wife,
Prophetess Esther Powell

Have you ever wondered what stops you from being who you are called to be and why you feel that you cannot stop doing what does not please the Lord?

If your answer is "yes," then *Spirits that Fight Against the Kingdom of God* is a must-read book for you. As the Goodman Twins, we are Prophetess Dr. Amber and Prophetess Dr. Ashley–the spiritual twin daughters of Overseer, Prophet Daniel Powell, Sr. We have been taught and trained by the Holy Spirit through this righteous man of God's teachings and impartations.

We are witnesses to the glory of God and the powerful anointing upon Prophet Powell, Sr.'s life. The oil released from him is so rich and just to receive his counsel, to hear him minister, or to read any of his books will cause you to revere God.

We believe this book is a blessing birthed right out of heaven and will be a blessing to the Body of Christ and even those who have yet to know about the King of all kings - Jesus Christ. This book has revealed to us many spirits that have attacked us, but through the writing of Overseer Prophet Daniel Powell, Sr. we know how to locate and identify the plans of these demonic spirits. The importance of willing to submit to God's perfect will, and to continuously be obedient to the word of God. May you be blessed as you turn the pages of this book in Jesus' name, amen.

Prophetess Dr. Ashley Goodman & Prophetess Dr. Amber Goodman of Heaven to Earth Worship Center Tampa, FL

SPIRIT OF ABOMINATION

Deuteronomy 22:5 (NKJV), "A woman shall not wear anything that pertains to a man, nor shall a man put on a woman's garment, for all who do so are an abomination to the Lord your God."

This is not directed toward fashion, but rather this refers to the practice of cross-dressing, as transvestites do; a sexual behavior, which is unnatural just as is homosexuality. This is not God and has never been God. Jesus loves us all, but He does not love the spirit of abomination.

SPIRIT OF ANANIAS AND SAPPHIRA

Do we have the spirit of Ananias and Sapphira?

I greet you in the grace and joy and peace of our Lord Jesus Christ. There are people in the church that have the same spirit as Ananias and his wife, Sapphira. This is serious. People are walking in the spirit of dishonesty, and deceitfulness is intentional concealment or misrepresentation of the truth. Or, doing the opposite of what one says or portends. This is not the Spirit of God. These people don't have the same heart or soul as the other believers. All believers should have the same heart, soul, or mind, isn't this something {all believers}?

If there are ten thousand believers, all of them have only one heart and one soul. They don't have ten thousand hearts or ten thousand souls, they only have one heart and one soul. When we have the same heart and soul as Jesus Christ and God the Father, we then know that what we own is not our own, but it all belongs to God the Father. When we have this revelation, we have no problem with giving to Jesus' ministry.

It will take the people of God to back Jesus' ministry. The word of God says that when believers give like this, they lack nothing. This is so powerful when we learn to give greatly as these believers did, we too will lack nothing. This means that there will be no more poverty in our life. Yes, they gave of their possessions, but to God, not man. God supplied all their needs. They had no lack. Where there is no lack, there's no poverty, that's powerful.

This is a mystery: when we don't give like this, we will lack something, and then comes the spirit of poverty. People of God, if we want to have no more lack in our life, no more poverty in our life, we must give our way out. The Word of God says that our God shall supply all our needs according to His riches and glory by Christ Jesus. The Word of God says give and He will [give back]. That's one blessing, then He said He will press that down and shake it together, and it will run over. Then, if this is not enough, God said that He will cause men to give to your bosom.

Wow, we all should believe this. This is the Word of God, so why are we not doing as the Word of God says? This sin that Ananias and Sapphira committed was not stinginess or holding back part of their money, they could have chosen whether or not to sell the land and how much to give. Ananias never said anything when Peter asked him about what he had sold, but it was what he did not say, what he said.

Their sin was not lying to man, but to the Holy Spirit. If you have lied to the Holy Spirit, then you are walking in the spirit of Ananias and Sapphira. Now they said that they gave the whole amount, but holding back some for themselves [they didn't trust God], trying to make themselves appear more generous than they really were doing. Does this sound like someone you know?

And God judged them for this lie they told to the Holy Spirit. See, when we lie to the Holy Spirit, it will cause God to judge us. He's the same God yesterday, today, and forever. He still hates liars, and liars are people that are dishonest. This spirit and the spirit of covetousness are destructive in the House of God. It can even prevent the Holy Spirit from working effectively. All lying is a sin, but when we lie to try to deceive God, His Holy Spirit, and His people about our relationship with Jesus, we are destroying our testimony of Christ Jesus. It's all about Jesus, not us, but Jesus. God is going to judge His people for telling lies to the Holy Spirit. See, we are not lying to man, or our Pastor, or our Overseer, we are lying to the Holy Spirit. When God judged Ananias and Sapphira, it produced fear and shock among the believers, but this judgment of God made the people realize how seriously God regards sin in His church. Let this not be us, if so, God will give us time to repent. Please repent, and agree with the Word of God as He gave Sapphira three days to repent and agree with Him, but she agreed with her lying husband, and, she too, died.

I pray this will be a blessing to you all as it was to the House of God.

SPIRIT OF ANTINOMIANISM

The Demon of Antinomianism

This demon of antinomianism comes to suppress the truth, and Jesus is the Way, the Truth, and the Life. This spirit is attacking the kingdom of God, it is trying to suppress the Truth and overpower the Truth. This is not happening to the true believers, but to the ones that are playing church (the prophet, prophetess, evangelists, pastors, deacons, bishops, praise and worship leaders) that are not preaching the truth. Because they are not living by the Truth. This demon does not discriminate. This demon is real. It is telling God's leaders and people that they can live in sin as the world lives in sin, and still work in the gifts of God, and go to Heaven. This is a lie from the pits of hell!

Matthew 7:21-23 (NKJV), "Not everyone who says to Me, 'Lord, Lord,' shall enter the kingdom of heaven, but he who does the will of My Father in heaven. Many will say to Me in that day, 'Lord, Lord, have we not prophesied in Your name, cast out demons in Your name, and done many wonders in Your name?' And then I will declare to them, 'I never knew you; depart from Me, you who practice lawlessness!'"

These leaders claim feelings of intimacy with Jesus that matter, good works, and even miraculous ones, but only doing the will of the Father by the Holy Spirit is what matters. And not by the spirit of lawlessness that lives with the demon of antinomianism. You see, genuine intimacy with the Father means knowing God and being known by God.

This demon is trying to crush the Truth and true prophets must warn the people of God of this Truth. Antinomianism is a demon and it has been sent by the devil to oppose the word of God, the Truth. This demon is telling God's leaders and God's people to oppose the Truth, and that God's word should not control their life. This demon is talking to the people of God, and they are listening to and obeying this demon. The word of God says, "My sheep know My voice and a stranger they know not" **(John 10:5; 10:27, NKJV)**: so why are the leaders and the people of God obeying this demon? This is because they don't want to live right.

This demon also works in the spirit of lust and lust brings forth sin. This demon knows that if we obey the Truth we will be made free from the law, the curse of sin, and death; and who the Son sets free is free indeed. This demon is telling God's people that once saved is always saved and that they can live a life of sin and it does not matter because they will still go to Heaven (this is a lie from the devil).

That's why homosexuals, harlots, child molesters, liars, and thieves are sitting in the pulpit preaching the word of God, because they are controlled by the demon of antinomianism. This demon will have God's people to deny any need to live a holy or righteous life by being taught the Truth by the teaching of the Holy Spirit and by the power of God, and how to live in Truth. See, it's God's Truth that will make us free, amen. The demon of antinomianism is not from God the Father, this demon is from the devil and is trying to keep God's people bound in the curse of the law of sin and death. Church, we must stand on the Truth, we must abide in the word of God.

John 8:31-32 (NKJV), "Then Jesus said to those Jews who believed Him, 'If you abide in My word, you are My disciples indeed. And you shall know the truth, and the truth shall make you free.'"

This demon comes to keep us from the Truth and to cover up the Truth to make the truth seem like a lie, because it's the Truth that's going to make us free.

Galatians 5:1 (NKJV), "Stand fast therefore in the liberty by which Christ has made us free, and do not be entangled again with a yoke of bondage."

Christ has made us free, so we must stay free by being obedient and submitting to the Truth.

2 Peter 2:2 (NKJV), "And many will follow their destructive ways, because of whom the way of truth will be blasphemed."

When we follow our own ways: we are being led by the spirit of antinomianism right into destructive ways and incorrigible and reckless sensual indulgence spirits. Especially in sexual immorality, and the Truth is being blasphemed by the spirit of antinomianism. The Word of God says that we are in the world, but not of the world. These are worldly spirits and they should not be in the lives of God's people or in the House of God, and God is about to judge these people. The things of this world are incompatible with the Kingdom of God.

This demon has some of the people of God in a grip of terror and doesn't want to let them go, but the devil is a lie he has no power over God's people. A prophet must warn them that a true spiritual person acknowledges and obeys the authority of God's Truth that's in the word of God.

1 Corinthians 14:37-38 (NKJV), "If anyone thinks himself to be a prophet or spiritual, let him acknowledge that the things which I write to you are the commandments of the Lord. But if anyone is ignorant, let him be ignorant."

If anyone does not recognize the Truth, then the Truth does not recognize that man. For to know the Truth is to be known by the Truth and the Truth is the word of God. This is a warning that those who are stubborn will be disciplined by the Truth in divine judgment, let this not be us. Repent and live by the Truth; the Truth will make us free.

1 Corinthians 6:9-11 (NKJV), "Paul was telling the Corinthians, 'Do you not know that the unrighteous will not inherit the kingdom of God? Do not be deceived. Neither fornicators, nor idolaters, nor adulterers, nor homosexuals, nor sodomites, nor thieves, nor covetous, nor drunkards, nor revilers, nor extortioners will inherit the kingdom of God. And such were some of you. But you were washed, but you were sanctified, but you were justified in the name of the Lord Jesus and by the Spirit of our God.'"

We are declared righteous because of Christ's death, and He will also lead us into a Holy life. True believers are sanctified and justified, but we must let the word of Truth deal with this demon, because the present misbehavior of the people of God is not pleasing to God and must be corrected. Persistence in this demon would be an indication that their faith is false and that they have no place in the kingdom of God.

The only way for us to be free from this demon is by accepting and living by the word of Truth, and the Truth will make us free and will make us change.

SPIRIT OF ANXIETY

Philippians 4:6-9 (NKJV), "Be anxious for nothing, but in everything by prayer and supplication, with thanksgiving, let your requests be made known to God; and the peace of God, which surpasses all understanding, will guard your hearts and minds through Christ Jesus. Finally, brethren, whatever things are true, whatever things are noble, whatever things are just, whatever things are pure, whatever things are lovely, whatever things are of good report, if there is any virtue and if there is anything praiseworthy—meditate on these things. The things which you learned and received and heard and saw in me, these do, and the God of peace will be with you."

Be anxious for nothing: a person with an anxious spirit does not trust God. This means that they are always worrying. We shouldn't be anxious about anything, it does not help us. This will cause a spirit of depression that may cause us to draw back from Jesus. The Word of God says that when a man draws back, He has no pleasure in that man. Can we see how the devil will send an anxious spirit to us so that we will not trust God, and when we don't trust God, this will cause us to draw back from God, not man, but God? The true and living God that holds all of our blessings and our destiny.

His will for our life will be done, and all that God says that we can be and have if we don't draw back from Him. When an anxious spirit comes upon us, the Word of God tells us to be anxious for nothing, but in (everything) there is no restriction on applying these things: prayer and supplication with thanksgiving and letting our requests be made known to God. Look at this there is no drawing back from God when we do what the Word of God tells us to do.

These four things we must do when an anxious spirit comes upon us–the practice of prayer: presenting our requests in prayer with thanksgiving is the antidote and will deliver us from an anxious spirit; no one needs to pray for us: we just need to go to the Father in prayer and supplication with thanksgiving, letting our requests be made known to God, (I like this) and then the peace of God will come upon us (amen), and this peace will surpass all understanding and will guard our hearts and our minds through Christ Jesus (this is powerful). This is a direct answer to the prayer of an anxious spirit-to know that God heard our prayer and supplication and our thanksgiving God will send His peace to us to live with us and that anxious spirit will leave us in Jesus' name. Now that God has heard our prayer, we must have a life of obedience. This is the right response to giving us His peace: because now whatever things are true; whatever things are noble (honorable-worthy of respect); whatever things are just (righteous); whatever things are pure; whatever things are lovely; whatever things are of good report; if there is any virtue (power, faith) and anything praiseworthy—we need to meditate on these things and the anxious spirit will leave us. Look at this in v. 7, it says "the peace of God." Now once we do all that, this scripture says—now look at v. 9, it says, "the God of peace." These are two different things—the God of peace is a richer promise than the peace of God, but the God of peace fulfillment depends on our obedience to the Word of God. People of God, let's not take the anxious spirit into our present and our futures, but, in everything, let's pray with supplication and with thanksgiving, and let our requests be made known to God.

SPIRIT OF APOSTASY

The apostasy spirit is twisting the word of God! When people turn away from God's truth and embrace false teachings, the apostasy spirit is in operation, and God's judgment will be on those who apostatized in the past. People, this spirit is trying to take over the people of God by operating in leaders. This is a warning against false teachers. Having the right relationship between correct doctrine and true faith is so important in these last days. The truth of the Word of God must not be compromised, because it gives us the real facts about Jesus and salvation. God's Holy Scriptures are inspired by God and should never be twisted or changed. See, this is what the spirit of apostasy does; it twists the word of truth into a lie, and when the Word of God is twisted, God's people become confused over right and wrong and lose sight of the only path that leads to eternal life (see, here is another spirit that's not God–the spirit of confusion). We as a church must see this spirit working in the house of God–leaders teaching falsely. We must pray that they get back on the right track by praying and calling them back to the basics of their faith. Then, the way to salvation would be clearer to God's people, or pray that God would move them (take them down)! Even some of our churches today have Godless or false teachers who twist the Bible's teachings to justify their own opinions, lifestyle, or wrong behavior. This spirit gives them temporary freedom to do as they wish, but they will discover that in twisting God's Word, they are playing with fire. God will judge them for excusing and tolerating and promoting sin! This spirit is in so many churches. This is sad, people of God, and the True and Living God is tired of this spirit, and He is about to deal with it!

SPIRIT OF NECESSITY / COMPULSION GIVING

2 Corinthians 9:7 (NKJV), "So let each one give as he purposes in his heart, not grudgingly or of necessity; for God loves a cheerful giver."

So let each one give as he purposes in his heart, not grudgingly, or of necessity, or of compulsion. When God asks us for an offering or to sow a seed, we must give what He has told us. He will place it in our hearts and we must give willingly. We have to stop giving with a spirit of compulsion.

The spirit of compulsion speaks like this: "they are always asking for money," "I don't see why I have to give all the time," "I don't want to give, but I guess I will so nobody will say anything to me about it," "they act like I don't have bills to pay," "I need food in my house," "my car payment is due," "I want to go out to eat, they must think I'm made of money," "I don't like this, that's all they want, money, I know I should have stayed home." We sit in the house of God thinking like this, and the devil is sitting back laughing at us and frustrating us in the house of

God. Which is a place where we should have peace, a place where we come to give our Lord glory, to praise His name. It is a place to enter into His presence, to see His glory, to hear His voice and His word, to hear the Holy Spirit, and to be moved by what He has to say to us, so faith can come to us, hallelujah! Hallelujah!

Bless the Lamb of God! It is where His glory is! Where we give Him praise! Hallelujah! People of God, when we give with the spirit of necessity/compulsion giving, we are saying we don't believe the word and we don't have faith in our God. Yes, it is man that is being used to speak, but it is God that speaks to us about giving, hallelujah! All He is trying to do is bless us, but He can't bless us, because we really don't want to give to God anyway.

That's giving in the spirit of compulsion, like you are being forced to give, pressured to give to God, or like God is demanding you to give, no— that's not so, the living God will never demand us to give to him, that's not god's character, that's why the word says that God loves a cheerful giver. How can we be cheerful when someone is making us do something? That's not how God's kingdom works, that's not the Spirit of God, the Word of God says that we should give willingly—this is what pleases God the Father. He says in his word not to give like we are being forced to give, that's why we are so mad in the house of God. As soon as praise and worship is over, we know the next thing is tithes and offering–this is a joyful time, a happy time, a time to be a blessing to my Lord, amen, hallelujah! Bless the Lamb of God! We should be so joyful because the living God says by the mouth of his prophet Malachi **(3:10-11, NKJV)**: "try me now in this" (I like that) "says the Lord of hosts, 'if I will not open for you the windows'" (more than one) "of heaven and pour out for you such a blessing," wow, hallelujah! That there will not be room enough to receive it, and if that's not enough, "and I will rebuke the devourer for your sake so that he will not destroy the fruit of your ground." That's the Word of God, listen to that authority that the Word of God has, wow. And we sit back with the spirit of compulsion being mad because the living God wants to bless us. How can a child of God get mad because God the Father wants to bless them with open windows, pouring blessings that we don't even have room for, and then (I like this) God the Father will rebuke the devil for our sake so that He will not destroy us? And when we don't give, or give with the spirit of compulsion, we are saying, "Lord, I don't need or want Your blessings." Can't we see the devil now? Are your eyes open now? In the spirit, we can see how the devil will use this spirit so that we don't walk in the blessings of the Lord, people of God. It is our season to walk in the fullness of our Father's blessings.

Listen to this, whenever the Lord asks us for an offering or a seed and something comes over us, and we feel sad or mad and say evil things in our hearts, and don't really want to give, but we give anyway, that's the spirit of compulsion. That's not God's Spirit. That's of the devil because God loves a cheerful giver. The devil doesn't love a cheerful giver, he hates a cheerful giver. But a cheerful giver and their offering or seed are protected by the Love of God because God loves not man, or the devil, sometimes not even the people in the House of God, but God loves a cheerful giver, amen, and that's all we need. Sometimes man won't love us, but God will always love a cheerful giver because He was and is a cheerful giver. He gave His Son Christ Jesus to us and He's given to us all things pertaining to this life, hallelujah! Amen. Jesus is Lord.

Sometimes we do give in the spirit of compulsion. Come on, let's be real with ourselves, not really wanting to give, but let God bless us, we will shout God's house down. Running and jumping with the fullness of joy, saying, "Thank you, Jesus! Thank you, Jesus! Thank you, Jesus! You are an on-time God!" Shouting, "Hallelujah, hallelujah, thank you, Jesus!" Telling everyone how the Lord has blessed us, and God looks down from heaven {shaking His head}, saying, "That's the way they should be acting when I ask them for My tithes and offering or if I ask them for a seed for My kingdom." People of God, can we see ourselves?

I believe that it is time for us, the people of God, to be delivered from the spirit of compulsion because God sees our hearts. Ask Him to deliver you, and He will. Ask Him for the spirit of giving and ask Him to teach you how to give freely and cheerfully, because through such giving, hallelujah [I feel God], in such giving, hallelujah, hallelujah, hallelujah, bless the Lamb of God. Hallelujah, hallelujah, thank you, Lord, hallelujah. In such giving, all of our needs and our wants will be met, and God the Father will be thanked. Yes, He will be thanked, yes He will be thanked, yes we will thank Him, yes He will be thanked, there's no other God like our Lord God Jehovah because His reward is with Him, and it's not small. It is a big reward because we serve a big and living God.

Proverbs 15:23 (NKJV), "And a word spoken in due season, how good it is!"

SPIRIT OF DOUBT

The surest way to have victory over the spirit of doubt is to remember all of your prayers were answered by faith in Christ Jesus. The more we pray with faith: the more we will see God answer our prayers by faith! And the stronger that a person's faith in Christ Jesus becomes, the spirit of doubt in that person's life becomes weaker.

SPIRIT OF FAMILIAR SPIRITS

Familiar spirits: why are you trying to find out your future by consulting witches and mediums? Don't listen to their whisperings and mutterings. Can the living find out the future from the dead? Why not ask your God?

Isaiah 8:19 (NKJV), "And when they say to you, 'Seek those who are mediums and wizards, who whisper and mutter,' should not a people seek their God? Should they seek the dead on behalf of the living?"

SPIRIT OF FEAR

The spirit of fear brings with it a lying spirit. In **Genesis 18:15**, Sarah lied because she was afraid of being discovered. Fear is the most common motive for lying. We are afraid that our inner thoughts and emotions will be exposed or our wrongdoing discovered.

People of God, lying causes greater complications than telling the truth. If your God can't be trusted with your innermost thoughts and fears, we are in greater trouble than we first imagined. For God knows everything and all things. God knows when we lie and when we tell the truth, even if man doesn't know, our God knows.

SPIRIT OF JEALOUSY

The spirit of jealousy fights the will of God.

This spirit will even try to stop the will of God in your life **(Acts 13:44-45)**. The entire city turned out to hear Paul and Barnabas preach the Word of God, but the leaders saw the crowds, they were jealous and cursed and argued against whatever Paul said. They were fighting the will of God for Paul's life.

This spirit will have you cursing and arguing at people that God is using because they are anointed and hearing from God and succeeding in life, ministry, marriage, their spiritual growth, and their faith, where you haven't. And this spirit will have you acting crazy. Because they have been receiving affirmation and honor from the Lord.

You know you have the spirit of jealousy living inside of you when it's hard for you to rejoice with the ones that are being honored or growing in the Lord and moving out doing what God is telling them to do. And acting crazy is your natural reaction because you are jealous. How dangerous and tragic this is when the spirit of jealousy tries to make you fight against the will of God in the lives of His people. If a work is God's work, rejoice in it. No matter who is doing it. If you can't rejoice with people when God has anointed them and His grace is moving in their lives, you have the spirit of jealousy and you need to ask the Lord to deliver you. This is a crazy spirit.

The spirit of jealousy will destroy you on the inside. King Saul's appreciation and love for David turned to jealousy as people began to applaud David's exploits. In a jealous rage, Saul attempted to murder David by hurling his spear at him. Jealousy is one step short of spiritual murder, it begins by destroying a person's spirit and character, then it manifests itself in harmful actions. You will want to fight them or key their car, lie on their husband, or their wife, or their children, or try to bring their ministry down. Beware of letting the spirit of jealousy get a foothold in your life. It will cause you to be spiritually murdered. It's time to get delivered!

SPIRIT OF LABAN

Laban spirit. This is also a selfish and self-centered spirit, and this spirit's goal is only looking out for itself, and the way it treats others is controlled by that goal only–to look out for itself, and this spirit will make profitable arrangements for itself at your cost. This spirit also is controlling, this spirit cannot bring itself to admit that it is wrong about anything. This spirit's job is to use people and this spirit is also jealous. For this spirit lives only to benefit financially from using you. But the person that walks in this spirit will never receive the full benefit he could have gained by knowing and worshiping the true and Living God.

The Laban spirit is so secretive and will deceive you with its trickery. Jacob had to deal with Laban; he was to work seven years for Rachel but was not told the oldest daughter Leah had to be married first, so Laban deceived and tricked Jacob to give him seven more free years of hard work. This spirit will make you work hard to meet its needs.

The spirit of Laban. This spirit manipulates and uses others for their own benefit. This spirit is unwilling to admit wrongdoing. But this spirit cannot stop God's plan. God has a plan!

SPIRIT OF LAWLESSNESS

God's Authority Can Only Be Worked by Righteousness, Not Lawlessness.

This is so true. So many of God's leaders and God's people think that they are working with the Spirit of the Lord when it comes to God's authority, this kind of power and authority is not to be played with. Some are playing and have tapped into another spirit and it's not the Spirit of the Lord. If you are not living a holy and righteous life and working in God's authority, don't fool yourself. Jesus will tell you in the day of judgment, *I never knew you.* "Not everyone that says to Me Lord, Lord, shall enter the Kingdom of Heaven, but He who does the will of God" **(Matthew 7:21, NKJV)**. There's a will of God, people. But what is the will of God for your life? Because "Many will say to Me in that day, 'Lord; Lord have we not prophesied in Your name, cast out demons in Your Name and done many wonders in Your Name?' And then I will declare to them, 'I never knew you, depart from Me you who practice lawlessness'" **(Matthew 7:21-23, NKJV)**. There are a lot of people that are working in the spirit of lawlessness, a rebellious spirit, a disobedient spirit, having no law doing whatever they want to, working in their flesh, their will is not the will of God by His Holy Spirit. **II Thessalonians 2:7-12 (NKJV)** says that "the lawless one will be revealed and the Lord will consume him with the Breath of His Mouth and destroy with the brightness of His coming." The spirit of lawlessness is of satan, and they come with power and signs and lying wonders and unrighteous deception because they didn't receive the Truth, they didn't love the Truth that they might be saved. They will be condemned who do not believe the Truth but had pleasure in unrighteousness—let this not be you. People, don't let down your guard; the same satanic power that will ultimately spawn this unholy deceiver (the devil) was already at work in Paul's day, and is at work in our day, but it is now restrained by the power of God. These lawless ones are false teachers who already trouble God's Church, let's not play with God, He's not ONE to play with. If this is you, repent we don't have time to play with God; Jesus is soon to come. And let Your Father God deliver you so you can walk in His will and work in the Kingdom of God effectively in faith and in His Holy Spirit and power and the authority and grace that God has given you. If we say that we are *the* righteous, then the profession of righteousness must be accompanied by concrete obedience, this obedience is faith in the gracious provision of God the Father and in His salvation. Concrete Holiness and concrete righteousness; even the ability to cast out demons or the gift of healing or other remarkable acts will not make one acceptable before God the Father.

People, we got to be Holy and righteous and not compromise with anyone, not even ourselves– that's Jesus' ministry. Clearly, Jesus believed that men could prophesy and do even more astonishing works while never knowing the God in whose name they were functioning. The Word of God tells us that Gift comes without repentance, what spirit are you working in? Just because you are calling out demons and doing astonishing works and healing the sick, you better know that you are working in the Spirit of the Lord, it's time out for playing. You think that you are okay with God because you are calling out demons, but demons must obey the Name of Jesus–that's the Word of God. But to work in this kind of authority in the Kingdom of God, God's authority, it's going to take great faith, do you have great faith? **Titus 2:11-15 (NKJV)**, "For the grace of God that brings Salvation has appeared to all men teaching us that denying ungodliness and worldly lusts, we should live soberly, righteously, and godly in the present age, looking for the blessed hope and glorious appearing of our great God and Savior Jesus Christ, who gave Himself for us, that He might redeem us from every lawless deed and purify for Himself His own special people, zealous of good works," this is a blessing. Can you see the blessing of our Lord, see Jesus redeem us from every lawless deed, (Amen) so if Jesus redeemed us from lawlessness, why are we then working in that spirit?

Speak these things, exhort and rebuke with all authority, let no one despise you, people, to hear the Spirit of the Lord is to obey Him and walk in Righteousness, and then the power of faith will be as unlimited as the power of God. That's why some have the authority to call those things to be not as though they were; that's power and authority, but there's a price to pay for that kind of authority. Have you paid the price for that kind of authority? **Mark 1:29 (NKJV)**, "Simon's wife's mother was sick with a fever, and they told Jesus; so Jesus came and took her by the hand, and lifted her up, and immediately the fever left, and she served Him." Look at the authority Jesus demonstrates by the Holy Spirit, His authority working look it this Jesus (taught) them with this same authority, also Jesus (commanded) demons to come out with the same authority and the demons obeyed Jesus, in healing the people who were sick Jesus proved His authority and power over sickness and diseases and Jesus was always praying and agreeing and walking in the will of

His Father. We say that we just don't have the time to pray, but we don't have time not to pray, Jesus found time to pray, and there He was told by the Father to work His will, that's what we need to do find time to pray, and seek the face of God and to find out what is the will of God for our life, and walk in the spirit of Righteousness so that we to can move out in this God kind of authority. Church, it's time.

God Loves Righteousness Not Lawlessness

II Peter 7-9, "and if he delivered righteous Lot, who was oppressed by the conduct of the wicked, so God will deliver us; the righteous from filthy conduct of the wicked." Be delivered from our filthy conduct. Nothing is too hard for God. The others, they do filthy things to each other, they have filthy thoughts from the devil– it's lawlessness, and we as God's people must be holy and righteous. The Word of God tells us to be holy because God is holy. Some of us are not holy because we don't want to be, and that's your own will, not God's will, and that's willfully sinning, and this is when we bring God's glory to shame. For the world sees us and knows we are not righteous.

SPIRIT OF LILITH (OWL)

Today I decree that in Christ Jesus we live to learn and we learn to live. For this is our portion. Lilith is the name of a female demon, "the night owl" **(Isaiah 34:1-14)**. She appears as a feminine demon; Lilith represents a harlot either naturally or spiritually opposing the righteousness of God. Lilith also means "she of the night" a spirit of lust that seeks to possess and seduce males to commit fornication with her, usually in the night with the promise of sensual pleasure, a night creature, this is a glooming spirit with a goddess like presence her name stands for owls and she has a perverse sexual appetite "ominous thing."

The owl spirit is a witchcraft spirit, specifically a soothsaying or occultist female. Owls represent the spirit of heresy and false prophetic, it is the mysticism of darkness **(Isaiah 34:14-15)**.

SPIRIT OF LOW SELF-ESTEEM

You do not have the spirit of low self-esteem because:

1) In Christ you are honored
2) Your Jehovah thinks highly of you
3) You are admired by your Jehovah
4) You are appreciated, valued, treasured, and cherished by your Jehovah God
5) You are of importance and respected by your Lord
6) You are highly favored by God and approved
7) You are blessed by your Jehovah
8) You are healed by your Lord
9) You are anointed by your Lord
10) You are the property of your Jehovah

Low self-esteem
We should not have it because God knows your name. **Psalm 40:17 (NKJV)**, "But I am poor and needy; Yet the Lord thinks upon me. You are my help and my deliverer;
Do not delay, O my God."

The leader of your country probably does not know you by name, let alone think about you, but the King of all creation, the King of all kings, the Lord of all Lords, the Ruler of the universe, Your Jehovah is thinking about you right now. (Bless the Lamb of God) allow this truth today to take your self-esteem to another level of glory, another level of anointing, another level of power, because knowing that your Jehovah always has you in His thoughts, perhaps you could do more to keep Him in yours. I will be delivered from that spirit of low self-esteem for it is demonic.

Jeremiah 1:6-8

A lack of self-confidence is a struggling spirit. Often people struggle with new challenges because they lack self-confidence. They feel they have inadequate ability, training, or even experience. The prophet Jeremiah thought he was too young and inexperienced to be God's spokesman to the world, but God promised to be with him. We must never allow the spirit of inadequacy and struggle to keep us from obeying God's call. He will always be with us. When we find ourselves avoiding something we know we should do, just be careful not to use lack of self-confidence as an excuse for this is a spirit. We can do all things in Christ. If God gives you a job to do, He will provide all you need to do it. There's a race we must run.

SPIRIT OF NAGGING

Nagging is a spirit, this spirit will give unwanted advice, and it's a form of torture. People nag because they think they are not getting through, but this nagging spirit hinders communication more than it helps. Do not be tempted by this spirit nor obey this spirit. It will take you into a destructive habit of hurting God's people. Stop and examine your motives, this spirit will have you more concerned about yourself: getting your way, you being right, than about the person: this is not the Lord's way of reaching His people, if you are truly concerned about God's people, surprise them with words of love be led by the Holy Spirit and by the wisdom of God not by the nagging spirit, for it's a foolish person that has this spirit, if this spirit is in you ask the Lord to deliver you, and you will be a blessing to the kingdom Of God.

SPIRIT OF OSIRIS

The Osiris spirit is the spirit of beer. When drinking beer this demonic spirit Osiris will unleash the spirit of anger; the spirit of aggression; the spirit of jealousy; lust; the spirit of adultery; and fornication in its drinkers. This is a demon and it is in the church. It is not God and never will be; our God is a holy God! This worldly god Osiris supplied its ingredients and blessed the production. We need to fight in the spirit and come against and bind this spirit off of our loved ones. This demon is causing God's people to fight and kill people, even as they drive. This demon Osiris is a generational demon, a curse that can only be broken by the blood of Jesus. This is our victory. **Romans 13:13 (NKJV)**, "Let us walk properly, as in the day, not in revelry and drunkenness, not in lewdness and lust, not in strife and envy." Some people are surprised that Paul lists jealousy and lust with the gross and obvious sins of drunkenness, adultery, fighting, and murder. When Christ Jesus returns He wants to find His people clean on the inside as well as on the outside.

SPIRIT OF PROMISCUITY

Proverbs 23:26-28 (NKJV), "My son: give me your heart, and let your eyes observe my ways. For a harlot is a deep pit, and a seductress is a narrow well, She also lies in wait as for a victim, and increases the unfaithful among men."

Here the wisdom of God is talking and telling us about a spirit of promiscuity, the harlot is like a deep well that is hidden until one stumbles into it. There are harlots in the house of God sitting in the congregation saying amen, lifting up their hands, and saying "thank you, Jesus" with their mouths, and we, the people of God, can't see them because they are hidden. And we won't know them until one stumbles into them. Church, this spirit will attack men, women, boys, and girls: this spirit is in the house of God and it shouldn't be taken lightly. Where the gatekeepers for the kingdom of God are: what are we praying and are we seeing as the church or are we just praying for ourselves? Church, it's time that we deal with this spirit by the power of God and the moving of the Holy Spirit, this spirit has pastors leaving the church saying that they will not pastor anymore, this spirit is attacking deacons, bishops, and prophets lying and laying up with immoral women, men, and prophetess are lying and laying up with immoral men and women. People of God this spirit of promiscuity is attacking our young people too, we must deal with this spirit: by the leading of the Holy Spirit.

The seductress is as a narrow well that has a narrow opening making it difficult for one to get out after falling in. The seductress who has the spirit of promiscuity is as a narrow opening when one walks or works in this spirit it's hard for that person to get out or to be delivered, because this is a strong spirit. It is easy to be led by the spirit of promiscuity, but difficult to rise from it because this is a spirit of a cult this is not of God, cults live by or work in this spirit that's why you will see that the ones that have this spirit of promiscuity hang together like a cult: so we are fighting the spirit of a cult that's the strong man.

Matthew 12:29 (NKJV), "or how can one enter a strong man's house and plunder his goods unless he first binds the strong man? And then plunder his house." So we must bind the cult spirit by the power of god that's the strong man and Jesus can take the house and that person will be delivered from the spirit of promiscuity and loose the spirit of righteousness whatever we bind on earth will be bound in heaven and whatever we loose on earth will be loosed in heaven amen. One can only be delivered by the power of God and the power of His might and the moving of the Holy Spirit. There's nothing too hard for God because Jesus is Lord of us all. You will change.

SPIRIT OF SCOFFER
The Spirit of a Scoffer is in the House of God

A scoffer is one that expresses insolent doubt or derision openly with no fear or faith in the Lord. **Proverbs 13:1 (NKJV)**, "a wise son heeds his father's instruction, but a scoffer does not listen to rebuke." A person that walks in the spirit of a scoffer has no wisdom and does not follow the leading of the Holy Spirit or the Word of God.

They are doubtful people, not faithful people, and they can't take a rebuke from leadership or from the Lord; is this rejecting His love? The word of God says that He chastises (rebukes) those that He loves, so it's hard for God to love a scoffer because that spirit keeps rejecting (chastisements and rebukes). The love of God and the Holy Spirit wants us to see this scoffer spirit; it is a spirit that mocks and will ignore correction indeed because this spirit hates correction, and it's in the House of God.

Proverbs 9:7-9 (NKJV), "Anyone who rebukes a scoffer will get a smart retort, anyone who rebukes the wicked will get hurt, so don't bother rebuking scoffers, they will only hate you, but the wise; when rebuked will love you all the more." The scoffer spirit ridicules the principles of the Kingdom of God; a person with a scoffer spirit can not be instructed nor trusted with the things of God. The person with a scoffer spirit has gone beyond a simple lack of judgment and has made a conscious decision for evil, living with the devil, having no faith in Christ Jesus, and living with doubt in his heart.

Proverbs 14:6 (NKJV), "A scoffer seeks wisdom and never finds it, but knowledge comes easily to those with understanding." The person with a scoffer spirit can't find wisdom because they cannot recognize the source (no faith) which is the fear of the Lord. The fear of the Lord is the beginning of knowledge; the fear of the Lord is the sort of reverence and respect that results in faith and obedience to the word of God with no doubting; because doubting is sin and sin leads to ungodliness and ungodliness leads us to a scoffer spirit.

SPIRIT OF SCHISM

Schism is a spirit that brings division between Christians, usually splitting one church into two. The sin of schism is committed by those who cause division by departing from Christian truth or behavior.

SPIRIT OF SELF-PITY

Self-pity spirit **(Job 10:1)**: When we face baffling affection, a human response is to feel sorry for ourselves. Our pain lures a spirit and the spirit's name is self-pity. At this point, we are one step from self-righteousness. This spirit will have us saying, "Look what happened to me, how unfair it is!" This is saying that God is unfair. Can you see this spirit now? When facing trials, ask, "What can I learn?" and, "How can I grow?" rather than, "Who did this to me?" and, "How can I get out of it?" Don't let suffering lead you to walk in a self-pity spirit.

SPIRIT OF SELF-CENTEREDNESS

The spirit of self-centeredness will bring us a loss of hope **(Psalms 100:3)**. God is our creator, we did not create ourselves. Many people live as though they are the creator and center of their own little world living without hope (this is being self-centered). Are you like this? Or do you know anyone like this? This mindset leads to greedy possessiveness and if everything should be taken away, the loss of hope itself. But when we realize that God created us and gives us all we have, then we won't let the spirit of self-centeredness take control over us. We will want to give to others as God gave to us, then if all is lost, we still have Christ Jesus and all He has given us. Let's not lose hope God can deliver us from this spirit.

Self-centeredness is a spirit and it results in jealous feelings **(Genesis 13:7-8)**. Surrounded by hostile neighbors, the herdsman of Abram and Lot should have pulled together instead; they let pettiness and jealousy tear them apart. A similar situation exists today. Many Christian people argue and fight, while Satan is at work all around them. Rivalries, arguments, and disagreements among believers can be destructive in three ways.

1) They damage goodwill, trust, and peace.
2) They hamper progress toward important goals.
3) They make us self-centered rather than love-centered.

Let this not be us. Jesus understood how destructive this could be in His final prayer before being betrayed and arrested. Jesus asked God that His followers be "of one heart and mind."

Self-centeredness

When you are too worried about what others think of you **(1 Samuel 15:30)**. Saul was more concerned about what others would think of him than he was about the status of his relationship with God. He begged the prophet Samuel to go with him to worship as a public demonstration that the prophet Samuel still supported him. If the prophet Samuel had refused, the people probably would have lost all confidence in Saul. Are you concerned about what people think about you? If so, then you are self-centered, ask God to deliver you for this spirit is not of God.

Self-Centeredness. Is it the opposite of true love? (1 Peter 1:22)

Real love involves selfless giving. Therefore, a self-centered person can't truly love. God's love and forgiveness free us to take our eyes off ourselves and to meet others' needs. By sacrificing His life, Christ showed that He truly loves us. Now we can love others by following His example and giving of ourselves sacrificially.

Self-centeredness is a character of poor leadership (1 Kings 12:15-19).

Both Jeroboam and Rehoboam did what was good for themselves, not what was good for their people. Good leaders put the best interest of the people above their own. Making decisions only for yourself will backfire and cause you to lose more than if you had kept the welfare of others in mind. Let's not be self-centered leaders.

Revelation Given on 10/6/2009

I greet the Church in the love of Jesus Christ. The Holy Spirit was telling me about a spirit and this spirit is the spirit of self-centeredness.

Some of God's people have this spirit of self-centeredness; this is not of God, and should not be in the House of God. We as the Church should not have this spirit, this spirit will fight the Grace of giving, and this spirit belongs in the world not in the Church. Yes, the word says that we are in the world, but not of the world, so this spirit should be in our soul. We will talk a little about a man that had this spirit his whole life, and his whole goal was to look out for himself; does this sound like someone you know? Or does this sound like you? It's the way we treat others that is controlled by this spirit of self-centeredness. Now Laban was the brother of Jacob's mother, Laban was also deceitful as Jacob was so deceitful walking with self-centeredness on the surface; we may find it difficult to identify with Laban, but his selfishness is one point that some of us have in common.

Like him, we often have a strong tendency to control people and events that lead to our benefit, our good reasons for treating others the way we do may simply be a thin cover over the motive of self-centeredness. We may not recognize our selfishness; always wrapped up in ourselves and not wrapped up in Jesus; can't you see this; these kinds of people are always talking about themselves and not about Jesus Christ or the work that the Holy Spirit is doing in the lives of God's people. This is the spirit of self-centeredness, however, one way to discover it is to examine our willingness to admit we're wrong when it comes to the word of God about how we should live, but some of the people of God say that they know God but they don't know God because they don't want to live as He tells them to live; through His living word. Laban could not bring himself to do this; if you find yourself amazed by what you sometimes say and do to avoid facing wrong actions in your life as a Christian, then you are on the right road back to your first love Jesus.

Although Laban treated Jacob unfairly, God still increased Jacob's prosperity and God will also increase the Church's prosperity. God's power is not limited by lack of fair play, He is God and He has the ability to meet our needs and make us thrive even though others treat us unfairly; that's the devil, as they also treat His Son Jesus Christ unfairly; what has Jesus done to us that we will treat Him unfairly like Laban treated Jacob? Jesus died once for us so that we may live in Him all that He has done for us has been for us and His Kingdom. Jesus is not self-centered, but we as the Church are still acting a fool by being self-centered. Let's not give in to the devil and play the same game over and over by being unfair to God, His Son Jesus Christ, His Holy Spirit, His people, and His Kingdom, but let's give unto the Lord and His work the Church is lacking because of people that are self-centered.

1) Those who set out to deceive people will eventually find themselves walking in deceit and being deceived.
2) God's plan and His will cannot be stopped.
3) They manipulated and deceived people for their own benefit.
4) They are unwilling to admit they are wrong.
5) They benefit spiritually and financially from deceit, but never received the full benefit spiritually or financially that can be gained by knowing and worshiping the living God; they will always have lack in their lives.

Let's pray for the Church of the living God, if this is you, repent and ask Jesus to forgive you and go on with Christ. If you know someone with this spirit then pray for them and love them and Jesus will be seen in their life.

May God bless you and keep you.

SPIRIT OF SLOTHFULNESS

The devil comes to steal, kill, and destroy. Hear wisdom. "He who is slothful in his work is a brother to him who is a great destroyer," **(Proverbs 18:9, NKJV)**. A slothful spirit has a brother and his name is "great destroyer."

SPIRIT OF TRUTH AND SPIRIT OF ERROR

I John 4

God's gift of His Holy Spirit, the spirit of truth stands in contrast to the many lying spirits that drive false prophets in the world to spread opposition to the truth. Beloved, do not believe every spirit but test the spirit, whether they are of God. So we cannot believe the false prophets, the false pastors, the false bishops, the false evangelists, or the false teachers. There are many and they will lie to us, but we can give their spirit a test to see if they are from God. Hallelujah wow! I like this.

We need to give these false prophets' spirits a test and see if they will pass the test or not amen. We need to test them to see if they will lead us in error. Or will they lead us into the will of God, into the love of God, into His holiness, or truth, in His way of life, or if they lead us to Christ Jesus then they are from God, amen? If not, then they are operating in the spirit of error and if you follow them then you too are false and a liar. If you don't know what spirit is leading you or them, then test it; amen.

The Word of God says that we can test these spirits to see if they are of God, hallelujah, bless the Lamb of God. I like that the only way that we will be able to see what kind of spirit is leading us or them is to give that spirit a test or a questionnaire because if that spirit is not from God it will lie. It will not tell the truth, amen. The devil is just the devil, he is a liar. When was the last time you gave a spirit a test? We can test the spirits, people of God Amen. If we want to see if it's the spirit of truth, or the spirit of error, but some of us know the spirit that is leading us is not the spirit of truth, that's why some of us don't want to give or take the test; because we know that the spirit will fail the test. But if you don't know, how would you know, unless you first test the spirit to see if it's from God?

If it's not from God then it's from the devil amen! We know the spirits that are operating in our life, our homes, our hearts, our mind, and our soul that are not from God. That's why we keep doing the same old thing over, and over, and over again. We just need to stop playing with God and get it right. Repent and ask the Lord to forgive us. Just get it right and fall in love with

Jesus all over again amen. The spirit of error has to get out of your life in Jesus' name! It's not from God. The spirit of error is from the devil, and it's leading a lot of God's people out of the peace of God, out of the joy of the Lord, out of the righteousness of God, out of the holiness of God, out of the blessings of God, and out of the will of God. It's even causing them to backslide. Pray, we have to pray and give up our lives to the Lord. We have to stop going the wrong way! It's time for the church to start going the right way and that is the way of Christ Jesus walking in the Truth, the Spirit of Truth and we will change.

SPIRIT OF YOGA

Yoga, a Shakti spirit, a serpent spirit, the destroyer

Shakti. It is the posture whose gestures motivate the practice of yoga. Shakti is linked to the pagan belief that something 'akin' to a coiled serpent lies at the base of everyone's spine. This is the devil, a spirit sent from Satan himself. That serpent constitutes the female energy in the body craving to connect with male energy a deity, (people of God let's not be fooled by this demon). In meditation, this energy unfurls as a snake, reminiscent of the snake charmer with the serpent in the basket. During yoga chanting the Shakti spirit awakens and begins with each gesture, position, and the meditation chant sound ---om----- to ascend up the spine and eventually unite with the male power of the Hindu and Buddhist deity Hive whose name means "destroyer!"

Psalms 17:4 (NKJV), "Concerning the works of men, By the word of Your lips, I have kept away from the paths of the destroyer."

Proverbs 28:24 (NKJV), "Whoever robs his father or his mother, And says, '*It is* no transgression,' The same *is* companion to a destroyer."

So we have people of God worshiping the destroyer as they are doing yoga. Let this not be you. If so, repent and turn back to the only true and living God.

The destroyer's job is to ruin you, to demolish you, to wreck and waste your life, to ravage your soul, mind, and spirit, to completely ruin you, and to do away with you worshiping the true and living God. To reduce you to nothing, take away your will to worship and live for Jesus and walk in the power of the Holy Spirit so that restoration will be impossible for you.

If this is you I pray and I come against this destroyer spirit in the name of Jesus Christ. This spirit will not overpower God's people and can't overpower God's kingdom. The destroyer's power has been broken by the power that's in the name of Jesus! I send the destroyer spirit back to the sea and dry places in Jesus' name.

To demolish and destroy something organized or structured is done by smashing it to bits or tearing it down. We need to see this spirit demolished. If you or another believer you know that is doing yoga tell them this spirit is not to be played with.

Apply the blood of Jesus.

Exodus 12:23 (NKJV), "For the Lord will pass through to strike the Egyptians; and when He sees the blood on the lintel and on the two doorposts, the Lord will pass over the door and not allow the destroyer to come into your houses to strike *you.*"

May God bless you and keep you.

WITCHCRAFT, SEDUCING SPIRITS

Witchcraft Is Not Our Portion. The Lord Is!

Isaiah 8:19 (NKJV), "And when they say to you, seek those who are mediums and wizards, who whisper and mutter, should not a people seek their God? Should they seek the dead on behalf of the living?"

Chain letters are not of God, this is superstition, a type of witchcraft, let us as true believers in Christ Jesus not take part in such darkness for this is of the devil. A typical chain letter consists of a message that attempts to convince the recipient to make a number of copies of the letter and then pass them on to as many recipients as possible. Common methods used in chain letters include emotionally manipulative stories, get-rich-quickly pyramid schemes, and the exploitation of superstition to threaten the recipient with bad luck or even physical violence or death if he or she "breaks the chain" and refuses to adhere to the conditions set out in the letter. Chain letters started as actual letters that one received in the mail. Today, chain letters are generally no longer actual letters. They are sent through email messages, postings on social network sites, and text messages.

Occult Practices

Black magic, fortune-telling, and the use of mediums and wizards. God has specific laws against the occult **(Leviticus 19:31; Deuteronomy 18:9-13)** because it demonstrates a lack of faith in God and many believers practice this today and say that they are saved! But it involves sinful actions, and opens the door to demonic spirits that will influence you to worship the devil so how can you worship Christ Jesus and the devil? It can't be done, the Bible says you will love one and hate the other one, which one do you love? And which one do you hate? Today many books, television shows, and games emphasize fortune-telling, séances, and other occult practices this is not of God don't let this desire to know the future or the belief that superstition is harmless it is not and it will lead away from Christ Jesus your Lord and king into condoning occult practices and occult practices are not of God they are counterfeits of God's power and have as their root a system of beliefs totally opposed to God. Don't be foolish!

Can I kick the devil? Astrology, the study of the planets and stars to predict the future, is forbidden by God, so why do we as the church do such things, knowing that it's forbidden by our Father God? **Isaiah 47:13** says that astrologers "cut up the heavens to follow their courses and assign their movements to their petitioner's future."

Witchcraft Is A Seductive Spirit

A seductive spirit has been sent out from darkness by the devil and has married some of God's people and this is a spirit that has also been attacking and living in and among, and fooling the people of God for a long time. This is an old spirit. This spirit knows your weakness and it moves on that weakness. This spirit is not of God; it is evil and it lives in darkness; it's of the devil. This spirit comes to bewitch and persuade God's people to live an ungodly life and to do all kinds of evil and wrongdoing, and that's sin in the eyes of God. That spirit is trying to entice God's people to lead them astray, to charm them, and to have them walk in a perverted way. Some of you are walking in this seductive spirit; it's witchcraft and not God. This spirit has been sent to bring the people of God out of the presence of God and out of the will of God. Look around your house and the House of God. Look at the people of God. Look and see in the Spirit. Can you see this spirit attacking God's people?

This spirit seduces the people of God to tap into something old, dark, and evil. The Word of God says that Jesus is the light of the world. God is not evil, He's a good God. They have tapped into something that's dead and old. They are practicing soothsaying and going to palm readers to tell them something good. But darkness can't tell us good things and can't give light. Evil doesn't have any good in it. This is witchcraft, people of God, this is not of God, nor His Kingdom. What voice are you agreeing with? Come out from among them, hear the voice of God, and agree with the voice of God. That's why some of you look so old and dark and you don't know why. It's because the devil has got the people of God consulting spiritists and mediums about their life. They are asking, "Will I get married? Who is my husband or who is my wife?" They are asking the witch about their job, their family, and their future. If you want to know this, ask your Lord Jesus Christ, the hope of glory. Talk to Jesus, He is your Lord.

Jesus Christ is Lord over our life. He has all our answers. He's our keeper, our Shepherd, our future, and our life. He's our song, our strength, and our righteousness. **Psalm 34:19 (NKJV)**, "Many are the afflictions of the righteous but, the Lord delivers him out of them all." Tell the Lord to deliver you. Say, "Lord, deliver me from this evil, and my soul shall be joyful in the Lord. I shall rejoice in His salvation." The Word of God tells us all that we need to know. He says, "Just ask Me and I will tell all things concerning My Kingdom." God is not a man that He should lie nor the son of man that He should repent. The Holy Spirit should be leading us, not a seductive spirit. The Word of God says that the Holy Spirit will lead us in all truth. Soothsayers, mediums, and palm readers are not leading you in the truth. They don't know the truth, they are false. Jesus is the way the truth and the life; no one comes to the Father but through Jesus. Soothsayers, palm readers, and mediums don't know anything about our Father God, nor His Kingdom, and they don't know Jesus Christ our Lord, the light of the world, the Son of God, the Lamb of God. This seductive spirit is of darkness. There is no life in the darkness of witchcraft, just death.

2 Kings 21 records that King Manasseh of Judah walked in the spirit of seduction. As king of God's people, he should have agreed and walked with God. But to the contrary, this king walked in agreement with the devil and was a witch, just like some of you. Manasseh was worshiping the stars. Some of God's leaders, pastors, and prophets, are reading horoscopes to find out how their day, their year, and their lives are going to be! "God is going to deal with them," says the Spirit of the Lord. Because they are telling God's people that it's all right to read horoscopes and to play numbers. That's not God and the blood is going to be on their hands. And they say it is okay, but that is a lie from the devil. This is witchcraft, it's not the Kingdom of God but the kingdom of the devil.

How can two kingdoms live in us? It can't be done. Choose one this day because the devil's kingdom is coming down by the power that's in Jesus' name. Hallelujah, bless the Lamb of God! You will know what kingdom you are in because the Kingdom of God is righteousness, peace, and joy in the Holy Ghost. That's the Kingdom of God. If you are not righteous or don't have the peace of God or the joy of the Lord or you are not filled with the Holy Spirit, then you are not in the Kingdom of God. If this is you, repent, and get back in God's Kingdom, amen. Leviticus 20:6, "And the person who turns to mediums and familiar spirits to prostitute himself with them, I will set My face against that person and cut him off from his people."

Consecrate yourselves, therefore, and be Holy for I Am the Lord your God, and you shall keep My statutes and perform them. I Am the Lord who sanctifies you." If anyone is reading the horoscope or the stars, they are a witch just like some of you. Repent right now to your Lord and your God that He may save you. God has blessed you and given you life and not death REPENT for the Kingdom of God is at hand, the living God He will forgive you and forget all of your sins. **Psalm 118:24** tells us this is the day that the Lord has made (not the devil but the Lord) we will rejoice and be glad in it, that's the Word of God. Because of Jesus' victory, God's people will turn the day of despair into a day of worship before the Lord. We don't need a witch's horoscope to tell God's people how their day is going to be; every day is a good day in Jesus because we serve a good God.

When we read the Word of God we should be agreeing with the Word of God not agreeing with a witch, amen. **Matthew 6:11 (NKJV)**, give us this day our daily bread so Jesus will give us a Word of life every day if we just ask Him; HALLELUJAH, bless the Lamb of God. Stop asking the witch for a word. How can two walk together unless they agree? How can a word from a witch tell us about a day that the devil had no part in creating? We are a blessed people. Every day is a blessing for us. **Psalm 30:5 (NKJV)**, "For His anger is but for a moment, His favor is for life; weeping may endure for a night, but joy (a shout of joy) comes in the morning." Bless the Lamb of God with joy, don't you know that we have God's favor for life, (do you agree with that)? Then say amen, and tell the Lord, You are a good God with joy, you know that you woke up this morning with God's Joy, bless the Lamb of God with a shout of Joy. Come out of darkness into the Light, Jesus Christ. I pray that all will be well in our souls, I pray that God's grace will always cover us and I thank the Lord and I pray that He will have mercy on His people.

A Seducing Spirit

This evil and dark spirit is working in the life of God's people and some of the people are rebelling against the will of God that He has planned for their life. I have talked to many people who are fighting this spirit and God showed this spirit to me whenever God shows me something in the Spirit He manifests it in the natural. Church, we got to pray, this seducing spirit is pulling people out of the Church, out of the will of God, the plan of God, and even out of His presence. What is so powerful is that they think that they are alright and they are getting darker and looking older; life is leaving them and the glory of the Lord is leaving also.

We as the people of God are asking the Lord about blessings and money and not about the people of God, and in our selfishness, the Church is being attacked by the devil and his dark spirits. The devil is a liar; the devil cannot and will not have the people of God. Jesus died for all of us and our victory is in Jesus Christ and in His blood. **2 Kings 21:8 (NKJV)**, "and I will not make the feet of Israel wander anymore from the land which I gave their fathers–only if they are careful to do according to all that I have commanded them, and according to all the law that My servant Moses commanded them.

Manasseh's reign is presented as the darkest period in Judah's history, but they paid no attention to the voice of God, and Manasseh seduces the people to do more evil. This spirit always rests on the one that has a door open and then he persuades the other people of God who already have something in their heart against God and His people and they too rebel against the voice of God. Can you see this spirit working in the House of God and resting on the people of God because they really don't want to live a Holy life, but they just don't know why they feel that way? It's the seducing spirit that is making them rebel against the voice of God. **(1 Samuel 15)** God told Saul to go and destroy the Amalekites, kill every one man, woman, infant, and nursing child ox, sheep, camel, and donkey also king Agag and take no spoils. But Saul let the king live, then the Lord asked Saul, "If I told you to kill the king and not to take the spoils, why did you not kill him, and why did you bring back the spoils? Why didn't you obey me; why didn't you agree with me; why did you rebel against My voice? I told the Prophet to tell you," but Saul said it was the people that took of the plunder. Saul is putting the blame on the people, but it was Saul that was walking in a seducing spirit; a spirit of rebellion is as witchcraft sounds like some of us always putting the blame on someone else when it's us. No one can make us walk in the spirit of rebellion (witchcraft) when we do we are agreeing and walking in the spirit of witchcraft and we say she told me to do that or he told me to do that; all along we were being persuaded by the seducing spirit to rebel against the voice of God because we want to and we are giving up our will to witchcraft. Let's repent people so that we can get back in the will of God. When someone tells us not to do something that we know that God told us to do and when we agree with them we are being seduced to rebel against the voice of God, the Prophet asked Saul why then did you not obey the voice of the Lord. The Prophet is saying why are the people of God disobeying His voice? I want you to be obedient to me. God told Saul, this is going on in the Church today we won't obey the voice of God; yes we give, but we are not listening to the voice of God. We are not obeying our Father when we are led by this seducing spirit; it degenerates us into an empty and often superstitious ritual when the people of God neither obey God nor ask to hear His voice.

1 Samuel 15:22- 23 (NKJV), "Has the Lord as great delight in burnt offerings and sacrifices, as in obeying the voice of the Lord? Behold to obey is better than sacrifice, and to heed than the fat of rams (for rebellion is as the sin of witchcraft); and stubbornness is as iniquity and idolatry because you have rejected the word of the Lord. He has also rejected you from being king."

People we can lose the glory of God and His anointing and God's honor when God rejected us for not obeying His voice. Sometimes we are like Saul; we fear the people and obey their voice. Let's repent and ask the living God to forgive us of our sins. You know the story God tore His Kingdom Saul and gave it to David let this not be us. Father God I pray don't reject us like You rejected King Saul, I repent for not obeying Your voice at times in my life. Thank you for forgiving us and forgetting all of our sins. In Jesus' name.

HOROSCOPE or HORROR-SCOPE

Exodus 22:18 (NKJV), "You shall not permit a sorceress to live." People, sorcery is not of God. Sorcery is the attempt to determine and influence the future through occult means, like reading horoscopes. This is strongly condemned by God. Why would the ones that say that they believe in the Living God and in His Son, Jesus Christ:
- Who knows all about us,
- And have given life to us through the Living Word of God,
- That can and will fulfill all of His plans for our life,
- The God that changes not,
- The God that's the same yesterday, today, and forever,
- The Living God that holds our life in His hand and knows all about us…and if we pray to Him, believe in horoscope?

He will let us know what is coming our way. The Word of God says we have not because we ask not, ask and it will be given unto you seek and you will find, knock and it will be open. If we need to know anything, all we need to do is ask the true and living God and He will tell us, or

Jesus will tell us, or the Holy Spirit will tell us. You might say "I know that"; then why are so many of God's people asking the sorcerer by reading horoscopes? This is a HORROR. This will cause evil spirits to come and talk to you and you will forget to talk to your Lord. You will try to live your day by what the sorcerers say–when God called the earth into being. They have no power. How can they tell you about your day when the Word of God says, "This is the day that the Lord has made, we shall rejoice and be glad in it." It doesn't say anything about reading a horoscope. Our future lies in God's hands alone.

Our Confidence Should be in Christ

2 Kings 21:6 (NKJV), "Also, he made his son pass through the fire, practiced soothsaying used witchcraft, consulted spiritists and mediums. He did much evil in the sight of the Lord." See people, this is evil in the sight of the Lord.

Micah 5:12 (NKJV), "I will cut off sorceries from your hand, and you shall have no soothsayers." God will clean His house of people who call His name Holy and have confidence in horoscopes and sorcerers.

God's salvation cannot come otherwise; only by stripping His people of all vain and false confidence. This is witchcraft and witchcraft is not of God. Behold I am against you, says the Lord of Host; I will lift your skirts over your face, I will show the nations (people) your nakedness, and the Kingdom your shame. I will cast abominable filth upon you, make you vile (despicable), and make you a spectacle.

Deuteronomy 18:9 (NKJV), "when you come into the land which the Lord your God is giving you, you shall not learn to follow the abominations of those nations (people), there shall not be found among you anyone who makes his son or his daughter pass through the fire, or one who practices witchcraft, or a soothsayer, or one who interprets omens, or a sorcerer, or one who conjures spells, or a medium, or a spiritist, or one who calls up the dead; for all who do these things are an abomination to the Lord and because of these abominations the Lord your God drives them out from before you. You shall be blameless (perfect) before the Lord your God. For these nations (people) which you will dispossess listened to soothsayers and diviners; but as for you, the Lord your God has not appointed such for you."

Anticipating the instruction from HOROSCOPES or HORROR-SCOPES, God forbids all these attempts to discern the future or the pass through the occult, as well as resorting to sorcery and witchcraft. This is a detestable character and not the character of Christ Jesus. I pray that the fear of God comes back into the hearts of His people and that we, as the people of God, get things right in their life. If God's Word made you mad, then you just might be a witch, a sorcerer, a soothsayer, or one that reads and believes and lives by reading the HORROR-SCOPE. Repent and come back to Jesus. Jesus will forgive you and forget your sins because He loves you.

GOD'S THOUGHTS AND HIS WAYS ARE NOT LIKE OURS

Isaiah 55:8-9 (NKJV), "For My thoughts *are* not your thoughts, Nor *are* your ways My ways," says the Lord. "For *as* the heavens are higher than the earth, So are My ways higher than your ways, And My thoughts than your thoughts."

We sometimes plan our life our way and not God's way, and when we plan our life, it will come to nothing. **Proverbs 16:1 (NKJV)**, "the preparations (plans) of the heart belong to man, but the answer of the tongue is from the Lord." God's way comes from His answer (His word is the decision). His word is the real power that shapes events in our life. The Holy Spirit wants to talk about God's people reading horoscopes. Why do we do this? This is not God; this is of the devil it is evil. The devil does not plan our day; or our life, our day and life are planned by God. Horoscope or HORROR-SCOPES is not of God. God's word is powerful and living and working in our life. Why would we read something that comes from darkness to direct our day or our life? This is not by the Spirit of the Lord. This is our way, this is our thought, this is not God's way or God's thoughts. The word of God shapes the events of our life.

When we read horoscopes we have tapped into another spirit. **Proverbs 16:2 (NKJV)**, "All the ways of a man *are* pure in his own eyes, But the Lord weighs the spirits." When we read horoscopes this is our way and the word says that this seems pure in our own eyes, but this is not the way of God. We are able to rationalize almost any kind of behavior as they strive to justify themselves. God's ways and God's thoughts are His knowledge; this is a warning against such self-deception that the devil is coming after God's people. If you are reading horoscopes, these are not good works, and these works are being committed to the devil; we need to commit our works to the Lord. **Proverbs 16:3 (NKJV)**, "Commit your works to the Lord, And your thoughts will be established." This is why our thoughts have not been established; because our works have not been committed to the Lord. Our plans should be entrusted to the Lord and the principles of God's word. Not to the evilness and darkness of the devil working, by way of horoscopes; this is not God's way or His plan for our life.

This is the word of God. **Proverbs 16:6 (NKJV)**, "In mercy and truth Atonement is provided for iniquity; And by the fear of the Lord *one* departs from evil." Atonement has been made in mercy and truth for the people of God that plans their day and their life by reading horoscopes. This is iniquity–hidden sin and by the fear of the Lord, you will depart from this evil. **Psalm 55:19 (NKJV)**, "God will hear, and afflict them, even he who abides from of old. Selah because they do not change, therefore they do not fear God." My prayer is that the fear of God will come back into the hearts of God's people; in Jesus' name, amen.

About the Author

Prophet Daniel Powell, Sr. is a native of Miami, FL. There he met and married the love of his life, Prophetess Esther Powell, and through this union, the Lord gave them three children. They celebrate 42 years of marriage and joyfully share in the lives of 11 grandchildren. Prophet Powell is the Founder and Overseer of Faith & Works Outreach Ministries, Heaven to Earth Worship Center, and Open Heaven Academy located in Tampa, FL, knowing that "the gates of hell shall not prevail against the Church" (Matthew 16:18). The mandate on his life is to "PREPARE GOD'S PEOPLE FOR THE COMING OF THE LORD."

Prophet Daniel Powell, Sr. is under the international covering of K.K. Ministries, Overseer Apostle Kathy Kinchen. He has certificates in Prophetic Leadership and Organization from Omega Bible College.

The Lord addressed Prophet as having the keys to the kingdom, and selected him to walk heavily in the areas of the authority to call those things that be not as though they were; an anointing for the barren–spiritually, financially, and the childless womb; and great deliverance. Prophet Powell, Sr. knows the value of deliverance first-hand, as he boldly gives detailed accounts of his deliverance from the old man—his former lifestyle of drugs, guns, demonic oppression, prison, and the enemy's plot of self-destruction.

Prophet Powell, Sr. is assigned to the area of birthing churches and oversees ministries in Florida and Georgia. Overseer Prophet Daniel Powell, Sr. labors in local and international vineyards, teaching the foundational truths of Jesus Christ. Hear Ye, the Word of the Lord.

www.ingramcontent.com/pod-product-compliance
Lightning Source LLC
Chambersburg PA
CBHW071346110426
42743CB00044B/3093